D1561280

Uncharted, Unexplored, and Unexplained

Scientific Advancements of the 19th Century

George Eastman
and the Story of Photographic Film

Heritage Middle School
Middlebury, IN. 46540

Mitchell Lane
PUBLISHERS

P.O. Box 196
Hockessin, Delaware 19707

Uncharted, Unexplored, and Unexplained

Scientific Advancements of the 19th Century

Titles in the Series

Visit us on the web: www.mitchelllane.com
Comments? email us: mitchelllane@mitchelllane.com

Uncharted, Unexplored, and Unexplained

Scientific Advancements of the 19th Century

George Eastman

and the Story of Photographic Film

by Joanne Mattern

Uncharted, Unexplored, and Unexplained

Scientific Advancements of the 19th Century

Copyright © 2005 by Mitchell Lane Publishers, Inc. All rights reserved. No part of this book may be reproduced without written permission from the publisher. Printed and bound in the United States of America.

Printing   1   2   3   4   5   6   7   8
        Library of Congress Cataloging-in-Publication Data
Mattern, Joanne, 1963-
        George Eastman and photographic film / Joanne Mattern.
                p. cm. — (Uncharted, unexplored & unexplained)
        Includes bibliographical references and index.
        Contents: A complicated hobby — A childhood turned upside-down — Successes and challenges — Making money; and giving it away — George Eastman's legacy.
        ISBN 1-58415-258-3 (Library Bound)
        1. Eastman, George, 1854-1932—Juvenile literature. 2. Photographic industry—United States—Biography—Juvenile literature. 3. Photography—films—History—Juvenile literature. [1. Eastman, George, 1854-1932. 2. Inventors. 3. Photography—History.] I. Title. II. Series.
        TR140.E3M38 2004
        770'.92--dc22

                                                                                        2003024125

ABOUT THE AUTHOR: Joanne Mattern is the author of more than 100 nonfiction books for children. Along with biographies, she has written extensively about animals, nature, history, sports, and foreign cultures. She lives near New York City with her husband and two young daughters.

PUBLISHER'S NOTE: This story is based on the author's extensive research, which she believes to be accurate. Documentation of such research is contained on page 47.

The internet sites referenced herein were active as of the publication date. Due to the fleeting nature of some web sites, we cannot guarantee they will all be active when you are reading this book.

Uncharted, Unexplored, and Unexplained

Scientific Advancements of the 19th Century

George Eastman

and the Story of Photographic Film

*For Your Information

During the 1800s, it took a lot of equipment to take a photograph. Some photographers used wagons pulled by mules to carry their equipment.

1

A Complicated Hobby

George Eastman was a hard worker. He had to be. Ever since he was fourteen, he had been supporting his family. He was very careful with money, keeping meticulous records of income and expenses. In 1877, when he was twenty-three, Eastman heard that the United States government was thinking about establishing a naval base in Santo Domingo, the name by which most people called the modern-day Dominican Republic. It is located in the Caribbean Sea just east of Cuba. Eastman thought that buying land there might be a good investment. If the government did build the proposed base, he could sell the land for a big profit. He decided to go to Santo Domingo for a first-hand look.

Just like travelers today, Eastman wanted to take photographs of his trip. He knew very little about photography, but that didn't stop him. He bought a set of photographic equipment and started learning how to use it. In 1877, taking pictures was a lot different than it is today. It was much more complicated. The camera itself was a huge wooden box. That was just the beginning. Eastman also had to buy a tripod to hold the camera, glass plates to make the photographs, a plate holder, a developing tent, developing trays, bottles of chemicals, a nitrate bath, and assorted jars, dishes, jugs, and funnels. All the equipment weighed about fifty pounds.

Eastman complained about having to carry so much equipment. "It seemed that one ought to be able to carry less than a pack-horse load,"[1] he said. However, a pack-horse load of equipment was exactly what was needed to take photos in those days. Photographers had to treat a glass plate with chemicals and place the plate inside the large, heavy camera. Then the photographs had to be developed inside a dark tent right after they were taken. It usually took twenty minutes or even longer just to get a single photograph. This long and complicated process was called "wet plate photography."

Despite the difficulties, Eastman quickly discovered that he enjoyed taking pictures. He took lessons and read books and magazines about photography. He became so involved in photography that he never did make his trip to Santo Domingo! It was probably just as well. The U.S. government soon lost interest in establishing a naval base there. Eastman probably would have wasted his money if he had taken the trip.

His experiences convinced him that there had to be a better way to take pictures. The whole process was so complicated and expensive that ordinary people could not take up photography as a hobby. Eastman wondered if a new process could be invented to make photography easier and cheaper. That way everyone could enjoy it.

"At first I wanted to make photography simpler merely for my own convenience, but soon I thought of the possibilities of commercial production,"[2] Eastman later wrote. His hobby would soon become one of the most successful businesses in the United States. By making photography as simple as pushing a button, George Eastman changed photography—and countless numbers of lives—forever.

FYInfo

George Eastman's parents were abolitionists. Abolitionists were people who opposed slavery. The Eastman house was a stop on the Underground Railroad and sheltered many runaway slaves on their journey to freedom.

The Underground Railroad was not an actual railroad. Instead, it was a network of people who provided an escape route for African-American slaves. These runaways hoped to reach "free states" in the north, where slavery was illegal. Some traveled even farther to Canada, where slavery was also against the law.

The Underground Railroad began in the 1780s, when members of the Quaker religion helped slaves reach safety in Canada. Between 1830 and the start of the Civil War in 1861, thousands of slaves traveled the Underground Railroad to freedom.

Most escaped slaves, or "passengers," traveled at night. They used the North Star to guide them in the right direction. Along the route, "conductors" (abolitionists or free former slaves) helped them find their way. The runaways stayed at "stations" during the day. A station might be a barn, a shed, or a house. Many houses on the Underground Railroad had secret passages and hidden rooms where slaves could stay until it was safe to move on.

Traveling on the Underground Railroad was dangerous for everybody involved. Runaways could be arrested, sent back to slavery, or even killed. Conductors could be arrested for helping a runway slave. Conductors and passengers were also hunted by slave catchers hired by slave owners to return escaped slaves, dead or alive.

Besides helping slaves reach freedom, the Underground Railroad also increased northern awareness of how terrible slavery was. As more northerners became involved in abolitionist activity, the southern states grew increasingly angry at their attitude. Many southerners did not want people in other states or in the federal government telling them what to do. This argument eventually led to the Civil War.

9

about 1880

Eastman about 1880, around the time he started his own photography business.

2

A Childhood Turned Upside-Down

George Eastman was born on July 12, 1854 on the family farm in Waterville, New York. The boy was named after his father, George Washington Eastman. The elder Eastman had grown up on a farm near Waterville. Later, he started the Eastman Commercial College in Rochester, New York. Students at the school learned bookkeeping, spelling, penmanship, and other skills that office workers needed. George's father also wrote several textbooks used at the school.

George Eastman's mother was Maria Kilbourn Eastman. She too had grown up on a farm, and had known her husband ever since they were children. In 1844, George W. and Maria married and settled in Rochester. Five years later they moved back to Waterville and bought the farm where George was born.

By that time, Maria had already given birth to three children. George's sister Ellen Maria was born in 1845. In 1850, another daughter, Emma Kate, was born. Emma Kate got sick with polio when she was a toddler. The disease twisted her arm, wrist, and one foot. She spent most of her life in a wheelchair. In 1852, Maria had a baby boy, but this child died soon after birth.

The farm where George spent his first years was filled with rose gardens and fruit trees. The family sold the pears, apples, cherries, and flowers they grew. Eastman's father spent the week at his school in Rochester and only came home on weekends and vacations. It was a trip of more than 100 miles. Despite his frequent absences, the Eastmans were a happy family.

George Washington Eastman raised his children with a strong sense of responsibility. He taught his students to learn by doing, and expected his children to follow the same advice. "I wouldn't have a child of mine that couldn't do any sort of an errand after it was five years old,"[1] he told a neighbor. As an adult, his son had the same practical outlook.

The Eastman Commercial College was successful, and the family had a comfortable life. All that began to change in 1857. George W. became ill with rheumatism. He could no longer manage the long trips to Rochester and the work on the farm. In 1860, he sold the Waterville farm, and the family moved to Rochester.

Life in Rochester was very different than it had been in the country. Rochester was a busy place. The city lay on the southern shore of Lake Ontario and was one of the main stops on the Erie Canal. Most of the wheat grown in western New York was shipped to Rochester and ground into flour in the city's mills. Factories in Rochester made shoes, clothing, tools, and other goods. These were shipped from the city to places around the world.

The family settled into a house near the college. George W. continued to work despite his poor health. Then, on May 2, 1862, he died of what a local newspaper called a "brain disorder." He was forty-six years old.

Maria Eastman was just forty-one when her husband died. In spite of the success of the Eastman Commercial College, she found that there was almost no money to support herself and her children. She rented rooms in her house to boarders to establish an income.

George Eastman's mother, Maria. She was left to raise George and his two older sisters after her husband died in 1862.

Education was important to Mrs. Eastman. Even though the family did not have much money, she saved every penny she could to send her son to a private school run by a man named Mr. Carpenter. It was known as the finest school in the city.

When young George was fourteen, he decided that he should help support his family. Mrs. Eastman did not want her son to leave school, but he was determined. When a local insurance agent named Cornelius Waydell offered Eastman a job, he quit school to take the job. He went to Waydell's office every day except Sunday. From 8:00 in the morning until 6:00 at night, he swept the office, ran errands, kept the wood stove going, and did other small jobs. For this work, Eastman was paid three dollars a week.

He enjoyed working. Contributing money to the family made him feel important. He also enjoyed having pocket money to buy things he wanted. His favorite thing to spend money on was ice cream. He also bought nice clothes, and purchased books and magazines.

In 1870, Eastman went to work for another insurance agency, Buell & Brewster. He was given more responsibilities around the office and was soon making thirty-five dollars a month. He earned additional money by making little puzzles out of metal rings and selling them for ten cents apiece.

Eastman especially enjoyed spending money on his sister, Emma Kate, who was more affectionately known as Katy. Katy could not walk and had to spend the winters indoors because of her poor health. Eastman bought her presents and paid for carriage rides around the city as a special treat. He was heartbroken when Katy died on December 3, 1870. She was only 20 years old.

Eastman's other sister, Ellen, had married and moved away several years before. Now Eastman and his mother were alone in the house, except for the boarders that Maria still took in. Eastman was devoted to his mother. She would live with him until her death in 1907.

In 1874, one of his mother's boarders told Eastman that the Rochester Savings Bank was looking for a clerk. Eastman got the job. Within a year, he had moved up to bookkeeper and was earning $1,000 a year. That was a fine salary for a young man in those days, when $300-400 was the average annual wage.

Eastman had a comfortable life. A little over a decade after his father's death had left his family almost penniless, the young man was making a good salary, had a mother who adored him, and enjoyed attending lectures, concerts, and other events that went on in the bustling city of Rochester. Most of all, he enjoyed his new hobby of photography. By 1878, always on the lookout for new ways of earning money, he was ready to turn that hobby into a business.

Frock Coat

Until the early 1800s, clothing was made by hand. Then the Industrial Revolution introduced machines that would do the work of people. After the sewing machine was invented in 1846, clothing began to be mass-produced in textile factories. These factories allowed thousands of the same items to be made and sold in stores at inexpensive prices. New York City produced more than 40 percent of all ready-to-wear clothes in the country.

In general, men dressed much more formally during the 1870s than they do today. For fancy dress, they wore long coats called frock coats. These coats were cut low in the front to show off the shirt underneath. The front of a frock coat was often decorated with silk ribbons or braids.

For everyday wear, most men who had professional jobs wore suits. By 1875, a short, loose-fitting style of jacket with padded shoulders was in style. This jacket was more comfortable and casual than the frock coat. It was also easy to mass-produce.

Bowler Hat

Under their jackets, men wore a white shirt and a tie. The cuffs and collars of a shirt received more wear than the shirt itself. These parts were made separately so they could be taken off and replaced with new ones, rather than replacing the entire shirt.

Hats were another important part of a man's wardrobe. Men were rarely seen in public without one. Middle- and upper-class men usually wore rounded hats called bowlers. Working-class men wore simple cloth caps.

Boys dressed like little adults. Very young boys usually wore short pants or knickers and a loose-fitting shirt with a jacket. When a boy was old enough to go to school, he usually began wearing long pants. Infant and toddler boys often wore dresses!

Leonardo da Vinci invented the first camera in 1490. He called his idea the *camera obscura*.

3

Successes and Challenges

Photography had only been around for about fifty years when George Eastman began taking pictures. Leonardo da Vinci, an artist and inventor who lived in Italy during the fifteenth century, had come up with the idea of a camera hundreds of years earlier. Da Vinci discovered that a small hole in one wall of a dark, enclosed room created a smaller, upside-down image of an exterior scene on the opposite wall of the room. He called his idea the *camera obscura*, from two Latin words that mean "room" and "dark" respectively. So our modern word camera literally means "room."

The main value of the camera obscura was to make it easier for artists to trace the images and improve the accuracy of their drawing. But there were many desirable scenes that were located far away from any rooms. So it didn't take long for artists to build miniature rooms, or boxes, that they could take wherever they wanted to. Some of these boxes were only a foot or two on each side. Even though such a box was no longer room-sized, it was still called a camera obscura.

As the nineteenth century began, more and more people began wanting artistic images to decorate their homes. They didn't have the time or the money to spend on drawings. It didn't take long for an alternative to appear.

A French chemist named Joseph Niepce took the world's first photograph (shown here) in 1826. The photo showed the view from a window of his estate in Saint-Loup-de-Varennes, France.

In 1826, a French chemist named Joseph Niepce placed a metal plate treated with chemicals inside a camera obscura to capture the image of the landscape outside the window of the room. Over a period of eight hours, the action of the sunlight on the chemicals created history's first photograph. Niepce called it a heliograph, which comes from two Greek words: *helios*, or sun, and *graph*, or writing.

Soon he began working with another Frenchman, Louis Daguerre, to try to improve the process and speed it up so they could make images of people. Niepce died in 1833 but his son Isidore continued the partnership. By 1839, they had created a type of image made on copper sheets coated with silver. These images became known as daguerreo-types and were quite popular during the middle part of the 1800s. The year 1839 was also significant because Sir John Herschel coined the word *photography*, from the Greek words for light and writing.

At first, only one photograph could be made at a time. Then, in 1841, an Englishman named William Fox Talbot invented the first nega-tive that could be used to make more than a single picture.

In 1851, another Englishman, Frederick Scott Archer, invented the wet plate process of film developing. This process was very complicated. First, a glass plate had to be coated with a sticky substance called collodion. Then the wet plate was taken into a dark room and dipped into silver nitrate to make the glass sensitive to light. The plate was placed in a holder and put inside the camera. Once the picture was taken, the glass plate was taken back into the darkroom and developed into a negative. Then it was treated with another chemical called a fixing agent to "fix" or keep the image on the glass. The whole process could take twenty to forty minutes. If the chemicals were not applied properly, or if the glass plate broke, the photographer had to start over.

Even though he had just started in photography, Eastman decided there had to be a way to make the whole process easier. He began reading everything he could find about photography. Soon he found an article in a British photography magazine that described a "dry plate" process for making pictures. It had been developed by an Englishman named R.L. Maddox. This process used gelatin instead of collodion to coat the glass plates. The photographer did not have to use wet chemi-cals or develop the dry plates right away. However, few photographers used the dry plate method, because the results were not reliable.

Eastman decided to make the dry plate method work better. After he came home from work at the bank each day at 3:00, he devoted several hours to experimenting. He cooked emulsion formulas on the kitchen stove. Then he coated glass plates with his formula and baked them in the oven. Finally, he took photographs of nearby houses to see how well his formulas worked. He became so wrapped up in these experiments that he barely ate. Sometimes he even slept on the kitchen floor. His mother worried that her son was getting too thin and would get sick. But he kept on.

"My first results did not amount to much," Eastman later wrote, "but finally I came upon a coating of gelatin and silver bromide that had all the necessary photographic qualities I was looking for."[1]

Even though Eastman had come up with a better way to coat the plates, he still had a problem. Each plate had to be coated by hand. At first, he used a teakettle to pour the hot gelatin onto the plate. Then he took a rod and spread the chemicals over the glass. This process was messy and slow. If he wanted to produce enough plates to create a business, he needed a faster way.

It didn't take him long to find one. He invented a machine he called a plate coater. Suction cups held a glass plate and pulled it across a roller. Each time the roller turned, it dipped the plate into the emulsion and coated the glass.

Eastman wanted to protect himself by patenting his idea. At that time, England was the center of photographic activity, so Eastman decided to patent his invention there. He crossed the Atlantic in the summer of 1879 and quickly received his first patent from the British government. The following April, he received a patent from the United States Patent Office.

Now he was ready to start his "biz," as he called it. He rented a room in a building just two blocks from the bank. After work, he rode his bike to his "factory" and got busy making plates long into the night. Eastman did everything himself. He cooked the emulsions, coated the plates, packed the plates, shipped them to customers, and kept track of all his sales and expenses. In between creating batches of emulsion, Eastman took naps in a hammock he stretched over the floor.

At first, Eastman did not have much business. To get people interested in his plates, he wrote articles and placed ads in photography magazines. Finally the owner of a photographic supply house in New York City heard about Eastman's work. The man was so impressed that he ordered more than $1,000 worth of dry plates.

Eastman realized that he needed to invest more money to make his factory larger. He had already asked one of his uncles for money. The older man thought his nephew's plan was too risky and turned him down. Then a Rochester businessman named Henry Strong heard about Eastman's idea. Strong had once been a boarder at the Eastman house and had stayed in touch with the family. He loved Eastman's idea and gave him the money he needed to expand. In return, Eastman made Strong his partner.

On January 1, 1881, Eastman's one-time one-man factory became the Eastman Dry Plate Company. Eastman used Henry Strong's investment to buy new equipment, rent more space, and hire workers. By September, the Eastman Dry Plate Company had sixteen employees and was making more than $4,000 a month. Sales got even better after a magazine called the *Philadelphia Photographer* tested Eastman's plates and wrote about their high quality.

Everything seemed to be going well. His new company was making money. He was earning more than $1,500 a year at his bank job. But he was in for a rude shock. When his immediate superior left the bank, Eastman expected to succeed him. The job went to a relative of one of the bank's directors. Infuriated, Eastman resigned. It was a daring step for someone who usually carefully calculated all his moves.

Even worse was in store. Early the following year, disaster struck. People began returning the company's plates, complaining that the pictures were foggy or too faint. Eastman could not figure out why his plates were suddenly no good. He recalled all the plates and gave his customers their money back.

Eastman closed his factory and performed almost 500 experiments to figure out what had gone wrong. The answer was still a mystery in March, several weeks later. Then Eastman, one of his assistants, and Strong sailed to London to visit the English company that supplied the gelatin for the plates. They discovered that the company was using a new supplier and the gelatin was no good.

By April, Eastman was back in Rochester and back in business. He replaced all the defective plates with good plates, even though it took almost every dollar the company had. "Making good on those plates took our last dollar," he said. "But what we had left was more important—reputation."[2] Eastman had also learned an important lesson. From then on, he tested all his supplies before he used them.

As the Eastman Dry Plate Company grew, Eastman thought of ways to make photography better. He realized that more people could enjoy photography if there was a way to replace the glass plates with something lighter. He began experimenting with paper instead of glass. He coated the paper with collodion. This worked, but the grain of the paper often showed through the picture.

After more experiments, Eastman came up with a solution of hot castor oil and glycerin that removed the grain from the paper. Then he coated the paper with collodion and gelatin, and finally applied a layer of emulsion. When the paper plate was exposed to light, it created a photographic image. Then Eastman soaked the plate in a hot bath to dissolve the gelatin. The finished product was a film negative.

Eastman patented his new invention, which he called American Film. He also patented the machine he invented to treat large rolls of paper. For the first time, film could be produced in long strips instead of on heavy glass plates.

Eastman realized that he had changed photography. At one time, only professional photographers could manage the complicated equipment needed to take pictures. Now many more people could enjoy photography.

"It gradually dawned on me that what we were doing was not merely making dry plates, but that we were starting out to make photography an everyday affair,"[3] he later said. His goal was "to make the camera as convenient as the pencil."[4]

About the time that he invented American film, Eastman heard about a camera designer named William Walker. Walker had designed a small camera that could be mass-produced. When Walker's company went out of business, Eastman hired him to be a partner in the Eastman Dry Plate Company. He also asked Walker to develop a new container that would hold Eastman's paper-backed film.

Walker came up with a light wooden frame with two spools. The film was wrapped around one spool, which moved it over the frame and onto the second spool. A key on the side moved the film as each picture was taken. Each roll of film had twenty-four exposures. The frame could be attached to the back of any camera.

Eastman was thrilled with Walker's invention. He changed the name of his company to the Eastman Dry Plate and Film Company. In 1884, Eastman placed an advertisement in many photography magazines. The ad promised that "shortly after January 1, 1885, the Eastman Dry Plate and Film Company will introduce a new sensitive film which it is believed will prove an economical and convenient substitute for glass dry plates both for outdoor and studio work."[5]

Eastman's film system won a gold medal at the London International Inventions Exhibition and received an excellent review in the *British Journal of Photography*. However, professional photographers did not want a new system of taking pictures. They were used to the old way. Eastman realized that he needed to find a new group of customers if his business was to be a success.

"When we started with our scheme of film photography we expected that everybody who used glass plates would take up films," Eastman later recalled. "But we found that the number who did so was relatively small. In order to make a large business we would have to reach the general public."[6]

Eastman hired a chemist named Henry Reichenbach to come up with a better film emulsion and find a material to replace paper as the base of his film. It was one of the first times that an American manufacturer had hired someone just to do chemical research.

Meanwhile, Eastman and Walker set about developing a small, inexpensive camera. Eastman hired three Rochester factories to build the parts, which included a wooden frame, a shutter, and a lens. The finished product was about seven inches long, four inches wide, and four inches high. It weighed only twenty-two ounces. The camera cost $25 and came with enough film to take 100 pictures. After the pictures were taken, the customer had to return the camera to the company. For a ten-dollar charge, the company would develop the film, place a new roll of film in the camera, and mail everything back to the customer.

Eastman wanted to come up with a special name for his new camera. He was successful—so successful, in fact, that the product name would eventually become almost synonymous with the term "camera" itself.

"I devised the name myself," Eastman later explained. "The letter 'K' had been a favorite with me—it seems a strong, incisive sort of letter. It became a question of trying out a great number of combinations of letters that made words starting and ending with 'K.' The word 'Kodak' is the result."[7] Eastman liked the word because it was short, easy to pronounce, and did not mean anything in any foreign languages.

In 1888, Eastman registered "Kodak" as a trademark. Then he turned his attention to advertising. He was determined to convince the American public that photography was a hobby anyone could enjoy. Eastman came up with the slogan, "You press the button, we do the rest," and used it to promote the Kodak camera.

Eastman's advertising campaign and his new camera were a huge success. For the first time, anyone—not just professional photographers—could take pictures simply by holding a small camera, looking through the shutter, and pushing a button. In less than a year, the company sold 13,000 Kodak cameras and processed 700 rolls of film a day.

Eastman did not stop with the huge success of the Kodak camera. Henry Reichenbach had been working to develop a better film. In 1889, he came up with a flexible, transparent film that had a nitrocellulose backing instead of paper. Eastman then created a way to mass-produce this film. Workers cemented together wide sheets of glass to form 80-foot-long tables. Nitrocellulose was spread over the tables and dried with warm air. Then a light-sensitive emulsion was spread over the nitrocellulose and dried to create film. Finally the film was peeled off the tables, cut into strips, rolled onto spools, and placed in storage containers.

Eastman was thrilled with his new product. He knew it would make the market for photography even bigger, because the film was easier to produce and develop. Eastman's transparent film also made it possible to create motion pictures. A series of images could be recorded on film and played back so it looked like action was taking place on screen. Another inventor, Thomas Edison, was already working on developing a motion picture projector. When Edison tested Eastman's new film, he knew his projector would be a success.

By now, Eastman's company had grown too big for its factory. Eastman bought fourteen acres of land near Rochester. On October 1, 1890, construction began on Kodak Park, one of the first industrial parks in America. Kodak Park included a new and much larger state-of-the-art factory, a power plant, and a laboratory. The grounds were filled with flowers, trees, and open spaces.

Late in 1891, Eastman was shocked to discover that four of his employees were planning to betray him. Henry Reichenbach, his trusted chemist, and three other men intended to leave the company and use Eastman's patented emulsion formula to start their own factory in Rochester. Eastman called their plan a "conspiracy." On New Year's Day, 1892, he fired all four men. The situation got worse when Eastman discovered that Reichenbach had allowed more than 1,400 gallons of emulsion to spoil. He had also sent almost 40,000 feet of damaged film to dealers. It cost the Eastman Company $50,000 to undo all the damage.

In 1892, Eastman changed the name of his business to the Eastman Kodak Company. The following year, he hired William Stuber to replace Reichenbach. Stuber soon came up with an emulsion that lasted longer than Reichenbach's. This meant that the film could be stored indefinitely.

Stuber was given a different challenge in 1895. That year, a German scientist named Wilhelm Roentgen discovered X rays, which could be used to produce images of bones and tissues inside the body. As soon as Eastman heard about this discovery, he asked Stuber to develop a way to make X-ray film. Soon afterward, Kodak began making special X-ray film for dentists.

Eastman was a smart businessman. He invested most of the profits from his business back into the company so it could continue to grow. He also paid his employees well and gave them stock in the company. In 1896, he shared a $178,000 profit with his 3,000 employees. In 1899, he gave all of them an extra paycheck as a bonus for their good work. He also handed out prizes to employees who suggested ways for the company to run better.

Eastman was never satisfied with his products. He always had his staff working to create smaller, cheaper, and simpler cameras. In 1900, he would produce a camera that changed photography forever.

Thomas Alva Edison

Few inventors have had as much influence on people's lives as Thomas Alva Edison. He was born in Ohio on February 11, 1847. He began school at the age of seven but lasted for only a few months because the teacher found his constant questioning disruptive. After that, his mother taught him at home and encouraged young Tom to learn on his own by reading library books. By the time he was twelve years old, Edison was selling newspapers to train passengers. He also read news reports that came into the train station by telegraph and printed them in his own newspaper.

Edison was always fascinated with machines. He became a telegraph operator at the age of fifteen. His first invention was a telegraphic repeating instrument. This machine allowed telegraph messages to be sent automatically.

In 1879, Edison invented the electric light bulb. This was probably his most famous invention. His other successes include the phonograph (1877), the first central electric power station (New York City, 1882), and the first motion picture camera, called the Kinetoscope (1891). In 1913, he combined two of his inventions—the phonograph and the Kinetoscope—to create the first talking motion pictures, though it would take more than a decade for them to become commercially successful.

Edison patented more than 1,000 inventions. His laboratory in West Orange, New Jersey, became a leading center for scientific research. Edison received many honors during his lifetime, including a Congressional Gold Medal "for development and application of inventions that have revolutionized civilization in the last century." By the time he died on October 18, 1931, he was one of the most respected and admired scientists in the world. Businesses and communities around the nation dimmed their lights to honor Edison after he died. Today he is still remembered as the man who was more responsible than anyone else for creating the modern world.

Eastman Kodak Co.'s
BROWNIE
CAMERAS
$1.00

Make pictures 2¼ x 2¼ inches. Load in Daylight with our six exposure film cartridges and are so simple they can be easily

Operated by Any School Boy or Girl.

Fitted with fine Meniscus lenses and our improved rotary shutters for snap shots or time exposures. Strongly made, covered with imitation leather, have nickeled fittings and produce the best results.

Brownie Camera, for 2¼ x 2¼ pictures, . . $1.00
Transparent-Film Cartridge, 6 exposures, 2¼ x 2¼, .15
Brownie Developing and Printing Outfit, . .75

The Brownie Book, a dainty, tiny pamphlet containing fifteen of the prize winning pictures from the Brownie Camera Club Contest, free at any Kodak dealer's or by mail.

EASTMAN KODAK CO.
Rochester, N. Y.

This ad for the Brownie camera introduced the public to a camera that was so simple, even a child could use it.

4

Making Money— And Giving it Away

Four years earlier, in 1896, Kodak had manufactured its 100,000th camera. It was a pocket camera that sold for five dollars. As usual, that wasn't good enough for Eastman. He turned to Frank Brownell, who had created many of Eastman Kodak's previous cameras and was one of his closest friends. What Brownell came up with would be second only to the Kodak name itself in terms of brand recognition. It was called the Brownie.

The Brownie sold for only one dollar. Film was just fifteen cents, and developing was only seventy-five cents. The Brownie was advertised as being so simple to use that even a child could take good photographs with it. The camera came with an instruction booklet and an offer for children to join the Brownie Camera Club.

The Brownie was so popular that it sold out immediately. Within a year, 250,000 people had bought one of these simple cameras. Many famous photographers started out with Brownie cameras.

Now photography truly was available to anyone. Finally, there was a camera that was small and light enough to carry, and easy to use. Taking photographs became an easy and enjoyable way to preserve memories. Instead of posing for formal portraits at a photo studio, families took pictures of themselves at home, enjoying everyday activities. People took Brownies with them on vacation. The word "snapshot" came into popular use, because people could just "snap" a "shot" and preserve it forever. Families kept scrapbooks with pictures of themselves, their homes, and their travels. The Kodak Company announced, "The Kodak camera created an entirely new market and made photographers of people who had no special knowledge of the subject and who had as their only qualification the desire to take pictures."[1]

By now, George Eastman was a millionaire. His success provided a comfortable life for him and his mother. However, it also caused a great deal of trouble for him and the company.

The first serious threat to the company came from a man named Hannibal Goodwin. In 1887, Goodwin had filed a patent application for his own transparent film. The Patent Office turned down his request because the application did not have enough specific details. When Goodwin did not submit a new application, Eastman could receive his own patent for film in 1889. Then, in 1898, Goodwin finally submitted a new application, which was approved by the Patent Office. This odd turn of events meant that Goodwin could accuse Eastman of patent infringement.

Soon afterward, Goodwin died in an accident. The Anthony Company bought his patent and offered to sell it to Eastman for a million dollars. Eastman was furious and refused. The Anthony Company quickly filed a lawsuit against Eastman Kodak.

A decade later Eastman Kodak was fighting with the United States government. In 1911, the U.S. Attorney General began investigating Eastman Kodak for violating the Sherman Antitrust Act. This act said that businesses could not "restrain trade" by putting other companies out of business to create a monopoly. If a company had a monopoly, it could raise prices and force people to buy its product because there were no other choices. Since Eastman Kodak controlled 90 percent of the photo-

The outside of the Eastman Kodak Company Building in Rochester, New York, in 1890. The building displays the company's slogan: "You press the button, we do the rest."

graphic materials market, it did look like a monopoly. Eastman Kodak had also bought other photographic companies and made suppliers agree not to sell their products to anyone else. The antitrust case dragged on for many years. Finally, in 1921, Eastman Kodak settled the lawsuit by selling some of its factories and equipment.

Meanwhile, the Goodwin lawsuit was finally decided in August, 1913. The court ruled against Eastman Kodak. Eastman knew the decision could put his company out of business. He agreed to pay the Anthony Company five million dollars in cash to settle the lawsuit. The money came out of his own pocket and saved the Eastman Kodak Company from disaster.

At the same time Eastman was fighting battles in court, he was also looking for ways his money could improve other people's lives. Unlike many other rich businessmen, Eastman did not want to start a foundation that gave away his money after he died. "Men who leave their money to be distributed by others are pie-faced mutts," he once said. "I want to see the action during my lifetime."[2]

Eastman was interested in helping people with dental problems. Both he and his mother suffered from bad teeth, and his mother had to have 15 of her teeth pulled during her lifetime. Eastman wanted to spare others, especially children, that suffering. In 1917, Eastman built the Alexander Street Clinic in Rochester. Any child could receive dental care there for just five cents. Eastman later started other dental clinics in European cities where Kodak had offices. He also donated five million dollars to start a School of Medicine and Dentistry at the University of Rochester in 1920. He later said that his dental clinics gave him "more results for my money than in any other philanthropic scheme."[3]

Many of the chemists who worked for him had studied at the Massachusetts Institute of Technology (MIT) in Boston. In 1909, Eastman donated $3 million to MIT's campaign to build a new campus. He asked that the school not tell anyone who had given them the money. MIT agreed, and listed the donor as "Mr. Smith." Eastman enjoyed the guessing games and arguments that followed until the identity of "Mr. Smith" was finally revealed a few years later.

Eastman donated a great deal of money to the University of Rochester. One of his biggest donations was to fund a school of music at the university. Music was very important to Eastman, and he wanted other people to enjoy it as well. The Eastman Theatre and School of Music was dedicated on March 3, 1922. Although the theater did not stay in business, the Eastman School of Music continues to be an important training ground for musicians today.

Another of Eastman's favorite causes was African-American education. Eastman respected Booker T. Washington, an African American who had risen from slavery to become the principal of Alabama's Tuskegee Institute, a training school for African Americans. Eastman agreed with Washington that students should improve their lives through training and hard work. Over the years, Eastman gave millions of dollars to the Institute.

Booker T. Washington was a famous African-American educator. Eastman greatly admired Washington, and gave large sums of money to his school, the Tuskegee Institute.

In 1924, Eastman gave a dinner party at his home. His guests represented MIT, the University of Rochester, the Tuskegee Institute, and the Hampton Institute, the school where Booker T. Washington had been educated. After dinner, Eastman signed documents that divided $30 million among the four schools. Afterward, he smiled and said, "Now I feel better."[4]

As with his business dealings, Eastman was practical with his donations. He never donated money to a school or organization without examining its financial situation first. Eastman also insisted that the recipient of his gift match it in some way.

His generosity even extended to the U.S. government. In 1917, the United States entered World War I. Eastman supplied chemicals to waterproof airplane wings and set up a school to train photographers to take pictures from the air. Kodak also developed an automatic aerial camera and a better gunsight for machine guns. Eastman was happy to assist in the war effort, even though he was in the middle of an antitrust court battle with the government. After the war, Eastman gave almost $183,000 of his earnings back to the government. He did not want Eastman Kodak to make a profit from the war.

George Eastman is shown here on the deck of a ship in the 1920s. In World War I, he provided supplies and cameras to the U.S. government.

What most people consider to be the first movie was The Great Train Robbery. *This twelve-minute film was released in 1903. Within a few years, movies had become a popular form of entertainment.*

At first, all movies were silent. The actors moved their lips, but their words could not be heard. Instead, dialogue was printed on cards that appeared onscreen.

The Great Train Robbery

Even though they had no spoken dialogue, silent movies were not entirely silent. They were accompanied by music played by a pianist or organist in the theater. These musicians made up the music as they went along, making sure that the style matched the mood and action onscreen. Some large theaters even had orchestras to accompany the films. These orchestras played music specifically selected by the filmmakers.

Rudolph Valentino

One of the most popular silent movie stars was Rudolph Valentino. Valentino was born in Italy in 1895. He moved to New York City in 1913 and became a professional dancer. In 1918, he began appearing in silent movies. At first, Valentino played villains. He soon moved on to playing romantic leads. Female fans adored Valentino's handsome features and dark, intense eyes. In 1921, Valentino starred in his most famous role, playing the title character in The Sheik. *His death in 1926 caused a tremendous outpouring of grief from women all over the world.*

In 1927, words were spoken on film for the first time when Al Jolson said, "You ain't heard nothin' yet" in a movie called The Jazz Singer. *Many movie stars panicked at the thought of being heard on film. Their voices were high-pitched, squeaky, accented, or just not appealing. Although the development of sound no doubt ended some promising careers, it was an idea whose time had come. The last silent film was Charlie Chaplin's* Modern Times *in 1936.*

35

Eastman and another American inventor, Thomas Alva Edison. Edison used Kodak film in his movie cameras. They are shown here working together on one of Edison's motion picture cameras.

5

George Eastman's Legacy

By the 1920s, George Eastman had made taking photographs an everyday activity. His work extended into other areas as well.

Thirty years earlier, Thomas Edison had used Eastman Kodak film in one of his own inventions, the movie camera. By the 1920s, movies were the most popular form of entertainment in America. Kodak produced most of the film used in making movies.

Eastman figured that if people enjoyed watching movies in a theater, they would like making movies at home as well. In 1923, Kodak produced the Cine-Kodak Motion Picture Camera and the Kodascope Projector. The products sold well.

However, Eastman was not satisfied. At that time, all commercial film was black and white. He wanted film to capture the colors of everyday life. He put his scientists to work creating color film. In 1928, the first Kodacolor film for use in movies was produced.

In 1923, Eastman had become chairman of Kodak's board of directors. He was now sixty-nine and felt it was time for younger members of the company to take over. "When I go I hope I shall have things in shape so they will go on just the same. What I would like to do is just fade out of the picture and not go out with a bang. There is a lot of young blood in the Company and I am trying to organize it so people will say after I am gone that the old man was not the whole thing after all."[1] Two years later, George Eastman officially retired from the company that he had begun.

Soon his health began to decline. He often had bad colds and got so tired during the day that he had to take naps. In 1930, he started to suffer from terrible pains in his back and legs. He also had trouble walking. Finally, his doctor diagnosed a condition called spinal stenosis. This disease causes the cells in the lower part of the spine to harden. It meant that eventually Eastman would have to use a wheelchair to get around.

He was devastated by the bad news. He had always been an active man. The idea that he would need others to help him made him very sad.

He also realized that the Eastman Kodak Company did not need him anymore. He did not even understand the complicated scientific processes that now went into making Kodak products. Although Eastman was glad the company would go on without him, he felt useless.

George Eastman had always been a practical man. He could not see the point of remaining alive when he could no longer accomplish anything or enjoy life. On March 14, 1932, he invited several friends to his home. They watched him sign a new will that left his fortune to the University of Rochester. After everyone had left, Eastman went to his bedroom and wrote a note which said, "To my friends: My work is done—Why wait? GE."[2]

Then he shot himself. He was 77 years old.

On March 17, all activity in Rochester stopped. Thousands of people lined the streets in front of St. Paul's Episcopal Church for Eastman's funeral service. The service was broadcast by radio all over the United States.

The films and cameras George Eastman developed changed life around the world. He invented new technologies that made photography simple enough that anyone could enjoy it. His inventions also led to the development of movies and X-ray film, which changed entertainment and medical science.

The Eastman Kodak Company continued to create new and innovative ways to use film. In 1935, the company introduced slides to the public with an improved color film called Kodachrome. These slides could be projected onto screens using the Kodaslide projector, which was also introduced that year. These inventions both used thirty-five millimeter film, which would become the standard size for most photography.

In 1963, Kodak introduced the Instamatic camera. These simple little cameras used film that was easy to load and unload. The public loved the Instamatic, and Kodak sold more than seventy million of them.

In 1996, Kodak pioneered the Advanced Photo System. This system produces high-quality pictures and allows users to choose different sizes and formats. Kodak also introduced the Photo CD system, which allows photographers to store images on a compact disc (CD) to create high-quality, long-lasting prints.

The biggest photo innovation of the last few years has been digital photography. This technology allows photographers to take pictures without film and download the images onto a computer. Using software such as Photoshop, they can easily make changes to their images and then print them out—which previously could only be done in a professional photo lab. Kodak is a major part of this market, producing cameras and media specifically designed for digital photography. The company continues to follow Eastman's ideal of making its products easy to use so people can have more fun taking photographs.

After George Eastman died, the *New York Times* wrote an editorial praising his life and works. "Eastman was a stupendous factor in the education of the modern world," the editorial said. "Of what he got in return for his great gifts to the human race he gave generously for their good; fostering music, endowing learning, supporting science in its researches and teaching, seeking to promote health and lessen human ills, helping the lowliest in their struggle toward the light, making his own city a center of the arts and glorifying his own country in the eyes of the world."[3]

It was a fitting legacy for a man who wanted to make photography available to everyone.

Eastman seated in the garden of his Rochester, New York, home in 1923. Eastman donated large sums of money to make his hometown a better place to live.

George Eastman loved to read the popular authors of his day. One of these authors, especially during the 1920s, was F. Scott Fitzgerald. Fitzgerald was born in 1896 to a wealthy family in St. Paul, Minnesota. His full name was Francis Scott Key Fitzgerald because he was a distant relative of the man who wrote the words to "The Star Spangled Banner." In 1917, Fitzgerald joined the U.S. Army and was sent to Alabama to train for World War I. There he met a young woman named Zelda Sayre.

Fitzgerald's first novel, This Side of Paradise, was published in 1920. It showed how people responded to the end of World War I by throwing themselves into the pursuit of pleasure. Its success gave him enough money to marry Zelda. She and Fitzgerald would become one of the most popular celebrity couples of the time. Zelda would become the model for many of Fitzgerald's female characters.

In 1925, Fitzgerald published his greatest work, The Great Gatsby. This novel tells the story of Jay Gatsby, a young man who falls in love with a married neighbor named Daisy Buchanan. To win Daisy's love, Jay becomes involved in illegal activities to finance an extravagant lifestyle. Eventually, Jay is ruined by his actions. The novel shows how pursuing wealth and power can destroy lives.

The Fitzgeralds lived in France between 1924 and 1931. During that time, their wild lifestyle caused Zelda to have a mental breakdown. She eventually died in a mental institution. Fitzgerald described her ordeal in his novel Tender is the Night.

In 1937, Fitzgerald moved to Los Angeles to write movie scripts. He died of a heart attack in 1940. Despite his short life and brief career, he is still considered one of the greatest American authors.

Chronology

1854	Born on July 12 in Waterville, New York
1860	Family moves to Rochester, New York
1862	Father dies
1868	Leaves school to work for an insurance agent
1874	Goes to work as a clerk at the Rochester Savings Bank
1877	Purchases photographic equipment for a trip to Santo Domingo
1879	Invents and patents a plate-coating machine
1880	Starts his own business selling dry plates
1885	Introduces American film; works with William Walker to invent a roller holder to advance film
1888	Invents the name "Kodak" for his film
1890	Begins building Kodak Park
1892	Fires chemist Henry Reichenbach and three other men after discovering their conspiracy to create a competitor; changes his company's name to Eastman Kodak Company
1898	Is sued for copyright infringement by the Anthony Company, which bought a patent from Hannibal Goodwin for a film similar to Eastman's
1900	Introduces the Brownie camera
1902	Donates money to the University of Rochester to construct science buildings
1907	Mother dies
1911	U.S. Attorney General investigates Eastman Kodak for violating antitrust laws
1913	Loses Anthony Company lawsuit and pays $5 million of his own money to settle the case
1917	Establishes Alexander Street Clinic in Rochester to provide dental care for poor children

1920	Establishes medical and dental school at the University of Rochester
1921	Settles antitrust suit by selling some Kodak factories
1922	Establishes the Eastman School of Music
1925	Retires from Eastman Kodak and donates $30 million to MIT, the University of Rochester, the Hampton Institute, and the Tuskegee Institute
1930	Begins suffering from spinal stenosis
1932	Commits suicide on March 14

Timeline of Discovery

1490	Leonardo da Vinci writes that a small hole in the side of a dark room creates an upside-down image of a lit scene outside the room. He calls his idea the camera obscura.
1826	Joseph Niepce places a metal plate treated with chemicals inside a camera obscura to create the first photograph.
1839	Niepce's son Isidore and Louis Daguerre create the daguerreotype, the first photographic portrait.
1841	William Fox Talbot patents the first negative.
1851	Frederick Scott Archer invents the wet plate process of film developing.
1871	R.L. Maddox invents dry plate photography.
1879	George Eastman creates a better dry plate process and invents a plate-coating machine.
1881	Eastman and Henry Strong form the Eastman Dry Plate Company.

Timeline of Discovery (Cont'd)

1885   Eastman introduces paper negatives and transparent film to replace glass plates.

1891   Thomas Edison invents the first movie camera.

1895   German scientist Wilhelm Roentgen discovers X rays, which can be produced on film; Frank Brownell develops the Pocket Kodak camera.

1900   Frank Brownell invents the Brownie Camera.

1914   Kodak scientist John Capstaff develops an early version of Kodachrome film.

1923   Kodak introduces the Cine-Kodak Motion Picture Camera for home use.

1928   Kodak produces the first Kodacolor film for movie cameras.

1935   Kodachrome film for color slides is introduced.

1942   Kodacolor negative film, which makes color prints, is sold commercially for the first time.

1950   Kodak receives an Oscar for producing a safer, less flammable film for movies.

1963   Kodak introduces the Instamatic Camera.

1986   Kodak produces the first megapixel sensor, which would later be developed into the digital camera.

1994   Kodak introduces the first consumer-oriented digital cameras.

1996   Kodak introduces the Advanced Photo System.

1997   Kodak introduces Kodak Gold film, which provides improved color accuracy.

2003   Kodak combines its medical imaging products with IBM Corporation's storage devices, forming a system to store and manage digital medical imagery at health centers.

Chapter Notes

Chapter One: A Complicated Hobby

1. Elizabeth Brayer, *George Eastman*, (Baltimore, The Johns Hopkins University Press, 1996), p. 26.

2. Ibid., p. 27.

Chapter Two: A Childhood Turned Upside Down

1. Elizabeth Brayer, *George Eastman*, (Baltimore, The Johns Hopkins University Press, 1996), p. 17.

Chapter Three: Successes and Challenges

1. Elizabeth Brayer, *George Eastman*, (Baltimore, The Johns Hopkins University Press, 1996), p. 27.

2. "George Eastman…The Man," http://kodak.com/US/en/corp/kodakhistory/eastmanTheMan.shtml, transcript, p. 3.

3. Ibid.

4. Ibid.

5. Peter Brooke-Ball, *George Eastman and Kodak*, (Watford, Great Britain: Exley Publications, Ltd., 1994), p. 20.

6. "George Eastman…The Man," p. 4.

7. Ibid.

Chapter Four: Making Money and Giving it Away

1. Peter Brooke-Ball, *George Eastman and Kodak*, (Watford, Great Britain: Exley Publications, Ltd., 1994), p. 24.

2. Elizabeth Brayer, *George Eastman*, (Baltimore, The Johns Hopkins University Press, 1996), p. 346.

3. "George Eastman…The Man," http://kodak.com/US/en/corp/kodakhistory/eastmanTheMan.shtml, transcript, p. 6.

4. Ibid.

Chapter Five: George Eastman's Legacy

1. Elizabeth Brayer, *George Eastman*, (Baltimore, The Johns Hopkins University Press, 1996), p. 498.

2. Ibid., p. 523.

3. "George Eastman…The Man," http://kodak.com/US/en/corp/kodakhistory/eastmanTheMan.shtml, transcript, p. 7.

Glossary

collodion	(kuh-LOH-dee-on) - solution used in photography to coat plates
emulsion	(ee-MUHL-shun) – light-sensitive coating made of mixture of liquids that do not dissolve each other
exposure	(ex-POH-shuhr) - a piece of film that produces a photograph when exposed to light
flammable	(FLAM-uh-buhl) - catching fire easily
gelatin	(JELL-uh-tuhn) - clear substance made from animal tissue
glycerin	(GLIH-suh-rin) - sweet form of alcohol
industrial park	large piece of land that includes factories or other businesses in a park-like setting
invest	to give money to a company in the belief that it will generate money in the future
lawsuit	legal action brought against a person or company
mass-production	use of machines to produce a large number of identical items at the same time
monopoly	(muh-NOP-uh-lee) - a company that has complete control of a service or industry
negative	(NEG-uh-tiv) - photographic film used to make prints
nitrate	(NYE-trayt) - a type of acid
nitrocellulose	(ny-troh-SELL-yoo-lohs) - cottonlike substance made from cellulose treated with acid
patent	a legal document giving the inventor of an item the exclusive right to make and sell it for a certain period of time
philanthropic	(fill-an-THROH-pick) – a term used to describe a person who donates money to improve society
stock	a share in a company
trademark	word, picture, or design that is owned by a company and can only be used by that company
transparent	(tranz-PAIR-ehnt) - allowing light to pass through

For Further Reading

For Young Adults:

Coe, Brian. *George Eastman and the Early Photographers*. London: Priory Press, 1973.

Lomask, Milton. *Great Lives: Invention and Technology*. New York: Charles Scribner's Sons, 1991.

Mitchell, Barbara. *Click! A Story About George Eastman*. Minneapolis: The Lerner Publishing Group, 1987.

Pflueger, Lynda. *George Eastman: Bringing Photography to the People*. Berkeley Heights, NJ: Enslow Publishers, Inc., 2002.

Works Consulted:

Brayer, Elizabeth. *George Eastman*. Baltimore: The Johns Hopkins University Press, 1996.

Brooke-Ball, Peter. *George Eastman and Kodak*. Watford, Great Britain: Exley Publications Ltd., 1994.

On the Internet:

American Museum of Photography
http://
www.photographymuseum.com

BoxCameras.com
http://www.boxcameras.com

Eastman Kodak Company: History of Kodak
http://kodak.com/US/en/corp/aboutKodak/kodakHistory/kodakHistory.shtml

George Eastman House International Museum of Photography and Film
http://www.eastman.org

National Inventors Hall of Fame: Individual Profiles: George Eastman
http://www.invent.org/hall_of_fame/48.html

The Wizard of Photography
http://www.pbs.org/wgbh/amex/eastman/

For Serious Researchers

The George Eastman House at 900 East Avenue in Rochester, NY houses scrapbooks, photographs, and correspondence documenting the history of the Eastman Kodak Company. Hundreds of boxes of George Eastman's business and personal correspondence were saved by his secretary. These documents are available in the George Eastman Archive and Study Center. There are also early motion picture films taken by Eastman. Eastman's original Steinway piano and music stands are used in museum musicals. The George Eastman House is a National Historic Landmark. The house and gardens were built by George Eastman and have been restored to suggest their original gracious appearance.

Index